EMMANUEL JOSEPH

Food Security and Biodiversity: The impact of agriculture on biodiversity and the need for sustainable food production

Contents

1

Chapter 1: Introduction to Food Security and Biodiversity

In a world marked by rapid population growth, shifting climatic conditions, and escalating environmental concerns, the relationship between food security and biodiversity stands at the forefront of global challenges. This opening chapter serves as a compass for the journey through the intricate landscape of how agriculture impacts biodiversity and the urgent need for sustainable food production.

Section 1.1: Setting the Stage

This section provides a contextual backdrop to the book, showcasing the fundamental importance of food security and biodiversity. It begins by defining food security, highlighting its multifaceted nature beyond mere sustenance. Food security is not just about having enough to eat, but also ensuring that the food is safe, nutritious, and accessible to all, irrespective of geographic or socioeconomic disparities.

Biodiversity, on the other hand, encompasses the rich tapestry of life on Earth, from the tiniest microorganisms to the largest ecosystems. It's crucial to elucidate the intricate connections between agriculture and the biodiversity of plant and animal species, as well as their ecosystems.

Section 1.2: Historical Perspectives

This section delves into the historical interplay between agriculture and bio-diversity. It emphasizes the pivotal role of agriculture in human civilization, from the Neolithic revolution to modern-day industrial farming. The chapter traces how the expansion of agriculture has led to widespread changes in land use, sometimes at the expense of natural ecosystems. Readers will gain insights into the agricultural practices of different civilizations and how they influenced biodiversity.

Section 1.3: The Modern Challenge

The section focuses on the contemporary challenges facing food security and biodiversity. It addresses the pressing issues of an ever-growing global population, changing dietary patterns, and the looming specter of climate change. Readers will come to appreciate the scale of the dilemma: how to produce enough food for a growing world while safeguarding the planet's biological diversity and vital ecosystem services.

Section 1.4: The Central Thesis

This section introduces the book's central thesis: that achieving food security and preserving biodiversity are not mutually exclusive but interconnected imperatives. It emphasizes that the pursuit of food security must go hand-in-hand with the conservation of biodiversity. Sustainable agriculture is presented as the keystone to reconciling these seemingly contradictory goals.

Section 1.5: Roadmap of the Book

Concluding Chapter 1, this section provides readers with a glimpse of the path ahead. It previews the forthcoming chapters, promising in-depth explorations of topics such as the impacts of modern agriculture on biodiversity, the role of agroecology and indigenous knowledge, policy and governance frameworks, technological innovations, and future challenges and opportunities in the realm of food security and biodiversity.

Chapter 1 serves as a compelling prologue to the book's overarching theme. It sets the tone for the comprehensive and multifaceted exploration that follows, preparing readers to understand, appreciate, and grapple with the complexities of the interwoven challenges of food security and biodiversity in a changing world.

2

Chapter 2: The Interplay of Agriculture and Biodiversity

In this chapter, we delve deeper into the intricate relationship between agriculture and biodiversity, understanding the ways in which these two crucial elements of our world interact and influence each other.

Section 2.1: Symbiosis and Conflict

This section explores the dual nature of the interaction between agriculture and biodiversity. On one hand, agriculture relies on biodiversity for essential ecosystem services, such as pollination, soil fertility, and pest control. On the other hand, agricultural practices have often been the cause of biodiversity loss through habitat destruction, pesticide use, and monoculture farming. It's important to recognize that this relationship can be both symbiotic and adversarial.

Section 2.2: Biodiversity in Agricultural Systems

Here, the focus shifts to biodiversity within agricultural systems. It discusses the rich variety of crops, livestock, and traditional agricultural practices that have been instrumental in human food production. Readers gain insights into how traditional and sustainable farming systems have incorporated biodiversity to enhance resilience and productivity.

Section 2.3: The Impacts of Modern Agriculture

This section examines the significant impacts of modern industrial agriculture on biodiversity. The intensification of agriculture, land conversion, and the widespread use of agrochemicals have led to the decline of many plant and animal species. The concept of "biodiversity hotspots" and the threats they face due to agricultural expansion are also discussed.

Section 2.4: Ecosystem Services and Biodiversity

Ecosystem services, the benefits that ecosystems provide to humans, take center stage in this section. It explores how biodiversity is intrinsically linked to ecosystem services, such as water purification, carbon sequestration, and climate regulation, and how agriculture can either enhance or disrupt these services.

Section 2.5: Case Studies

Real-world case studies offer a practical perspective on the interplay between agriculture and biodiversity. Readers will encounter examples of both successful biodiversity conservation within agricultural landscapes and instances where poor agricultural practices have devastated local ecosystems.

Section 2.6: Balancing the Equation

This section wraps up the chapter by introducing the concept of "sustainable intensification" – a strategy to balance the demands of food security with the preservation of biodiversity. It suggests that through responsible agricultural practices, we can optimize food production without causing irreparable harm to the natural world.

Chapter 2 acts as a bridge connecting the fundamental concepts introduced in Chapter 1 with the practical challenges and solutions discussed in subsequent chapters. It underscores the complexity of the agriculture-biodiversity relationship and sets the stage for a deeper exploration of how to harmonize these seemingly conflicting imperatives for a more sustainable future.

3

Chapter 3: Historical Perspectives on Food Production and Biodiversity

In this chapter, we embark on a historical journey to understand how human practices in food production have shaped and been shaped by biodiversity over time. This historical context is essential for appreciating the evolution of the intricate relationship between agriculture and biodiversity.

Section 3.1: The Roots of Agriculture

This section takes us back to the dawn of agriculture, exploring the transition from hunter-gatherer societies to settled agricultural communities. It discusses the origins of crop cultivation and the domestication of animals, emphasizing the coexistence of humans and biodiversity during these early stages of food production.

Section 3.2: Ancient Farming Practices

Readers are introduced to the farming practices of ancient civilizations. Case studies from Mesopotamia, the Nile Valley, and Mesoamerica illustrate the biodiversity-rich agricultural systems that characterized these early societies.

It becomes evident that ancient farmers maintained a balance between food production and the preservation of local ecosystems.

Section 3.3: Biodiversity in Traditional Agriculture

This section explores traditional agricultural practices from various parts of the world. It highlights the indigenous knowledge and sustainable techniques employed by these societies to enhance agricultural biodiversity, promoting the coexistence of a wide range of crop varieties and livestock within natural ecosystems.

Section 3.4: Early Agricultural Challenges

The chapter discusses the challenges faced by early agricultural societies, including pest infestations and soil depletion. It underscores the innovative methods employed to combat these challenges, often without compromising the rich biodiversity they relied upon.

Section 3.5: The Agricultural Revolution

This section explores the transition from traditional agriculture to the Agricultural Revolution, characterized by mechanization and the advent of modern farming practices. It reflects on how this transformation led to increased food production but also laid the groundwork for significant biodiversity loss.

Section 3.6: Lessons from History

In the final section, readers are encouraged to reflect on the lessons history offers. It underscores that throughout millennia, humans have practiced various forms of agriculture that harmonized with biodiversity. These historical examples provide valuable insights into how we might reimagine modern agriculture to better align with sustainable food production and the conservation of biodiversity.

Chapter 3 serves as a lens into the past, illuminating the diverse ways in which humans have interacted with biodiversity in the pursuit of food production. This historical perspective informs our understanding of the present challenges and offers inspiration for sustainable agriculture practices that can guide us into the future.

4

Chapter 4: Modern Agriculture's Impact on Biodiversity

This chapter delves deep into the contemporary landscape of agriculture, dissecting the myriad ways in which modern agricultural practices have influenced and, often, imperiled biodiversity.

Section 4.1: Industrial Agriculture

This section begins by examining the hallmark of modern agriculture: industrialization. It elucidates how large-scale monoculture farming, heavy machinery, chemical inputs, and genetically modified organisms have come to dominate agricultural landscapes. Readers will gain an understanding of the immense scale of industrial agriculture and its consequences.

Section 4.2: Habitat Loss and Fragmentation

Modern agriculture has been a major driver of habitat loss and fragmentation. This section explores how the clearing of vast swaths of land for agriculture has disrupted ecosystems, leading to the isolation of species and, in many cases, their decline or extinction. The concept of "agricultural sprawl" and its impact on natural habitats is discussed.

Section 4.3: Pesticides and Biodiversity

Pesticides have been a double-edged sword in modern agriculture. This section delves into the widespread use of chemical pesticides and herbicides, their effects on non-target species, and the emergence of resistant pests. It also touches on the role of neonicotinoids in pollinator decline and the impacts of pesticide contamination on aquatic ecosystems.

Section 4.4: Genetic Homogenization

The chapter discusses the homogenization of crop varieties and livestock breeds in modern agriculture. It explores how the emphasis on a few high-yielding species has led to a narrowing of genetic diversity, making food systems vulnerable to disease outbreaks and other unforeseen challenges.

Section 4.5: Water Use and Pollution

Modern agriculture's demands on water resources and the pollution caused by agrochemical runoff are covered in this section. The chapter delves into how the excessive use of water for irrigation and the contamination of water bodies with agricultural chemicals have far-reaching consequences for both aquatic and terrestrial biodiversity.

Section 4.6: The Role of Technology

Advancements in technology and their impact on modern agriculture are examined. The discussion ranges from precision agriculture and genetically modified crops to automated machinery. While technology offers the potential for more efficient and sustainable farming, its application can also lead to environmental degradation.

Chapter 4 serves as a sobering exploration of the challenges posed by modern agricultural practices on biodiversity. It underscores the urgent need for a reevaluation of these practices to mitigate their harmful effects on the world's ecosystems and find a more sustainable path forward for food production.

5

Chapter 5: Biodiversity Loss and Its Implications for Food Security

In this chapter, we investigate the consequences of biodiversity loss and how it impacts our ability to ensure food security.

Section 5.1: Biodiversity Loss - A Global Crisis

This section begins by highlighting the extent of global biodiversity loss. It draws attention to the alarming rates of species extinction, the degradation of ecosystems, and the consequences of habitat destruction, emphasizing that biodiversity loss is a pressing global crisis.

Section 5.2: Impacts on Food Systems

Biodiversity plays a crucial role in food systems. This section explores how the decline in biodiversity affects crop pollination, soil fertility, natural pest control, and the availability of diverse food sources. Readers will gain a deeper understanding of the intricate connections between biodiversity and food security.

Section 5.3: Vulnerable Communities

This section delves into how biodiversity loss disproportionately affects vulnerable communities, often in developing regions. It discusses how indigenous peoples and smallholder farmers are particularly reliant on local biodiversity for their food and livelihoods, and how the loss of these resources exacerbates food insecurity.

Section 5.4: Climate Change Feedback Loops

Biodiversity loss is intricately linked to climate change. This section explores the feedback loops between biodiversity decline and climate change, emphasizing how the two issues are mutually reinforcing. It underscores the urgency of addressing both challenges simultaneously.

Section 5.5: The Resilience of Diverse Systems

This section introduces the concept of resilience in food systems. It highlights how diverse, biodiverse agricultural systems are often more resilient to environmental shocks, pests, and disease outbreaks. Examples of diversified farming practices that enhance resilience are discussed.

Section 5.6: The Need for Ecosystem Restoration

The chapter concludes by emphasizing the importance of ecosystem restoration and the conservation of biodiversity to ensure long-term food security. It underscores the potential for rewilding and reforestation efforts to mitigate the impacts of biodiversity loss and secure the future of food production.

Chapter 5 serves as a crucial exploration of the dire consequences of biodiversity loss on our ability to feed the world's population. It underscores the urgency of preserving biodiversity as a foundational element of sustainable food security and highlights the interconnected nature of these global challenges.

6

Chapter 6: Sustainable Agriculture Practices and Biodiversity Conservation

In this chapter, we shift our focus from the problems associated with modern agriculture to the solutions offered by sustainable agriculture practices that aim to harmonize food production and biodiversity conservation.

Section 6.1: What Is Sustainable Agriculture?

This section introduces the concept of sustainable agriculture, emphasizing its three pillars: environmental responsibility, economic viability, and social equity. It explains that sustainable agriculture aims to balance food production with biodiversity conservation and the well-being of farming communities.

Section 6.2: Agroecology and Biodiversity

Agroecology takes center stage in this section. It explores how agroecological practices mimic natural ecosystems, emphasizing the importance of crop diversification, intercropping, and the integration of livestock. Readers will learn how these practices promote biodiversity in agricultural landscapes.

Section 6.3: Organic Farming and Biodiversity

The chapter discusses organic farming and its role in preserving biodiversity. It delves into how organic practices, such as avoiding synthetic pesticides and fertilizers, contribute to healthier ecosystems. Case studies of successful organic farming systems that prioritize biodiversity are presented.

Section 6.4: Permaculture and Sustainable Design

Permaculture principles and sustainable design are explored in this section. It discusses how permaculture seeks to create self-sustaining, biodiverse systems, often with minimal external inputs. Readers will gain insights into how permaculture principles can be applied to diverse farming contexts.

Section 6.5: The Role of Sustainable Fisheries

The section shifts focus to sustainable fisheries and aquaculture. It underscores the importance of responsible fishing practices and sustainable aquaculture in protecting aquatic biodiversity and ensuring a steady supply of fish for food security.

Section 6.6: Benefits of Sustainable Agriculture

Concluding the chapter, this section highlights the numerous benefits of sustainable agriculture for biodiversity conservation. It emphasizes that biodiversity-rich farming systems are more resilient to pests, climate change, and other disruptions. It also discusses the economic and social advantages of sustainable farming practices.

Chapter 6 serves as a beacon of hope, demonstrating that practical solutions exist to address the challenges posed by modern agriculture. It underscores the potential of sustainable agriculture practices to enhance food security while conserving biodiversity, offering a path towards a more harmonious and sustainable future.

7

Chapter 7: Ecosystem Services and their Role in Food Security

This chapter delves into the vital connection between ecosystems and the services they provide to support food security, underscoring the intrinsic link between biodiversity and our ability to nourish the world's population.

Section 7.1: Understanding Ecosystem Services

This section begins by defining ecosystem services, the benefits that ecosystems provide to humanity. It categorizes these services into four main groups: provisioning (e.g., food and water), regulating (e.g., climate and disease control), supporting (e.g., nutrient cycles), and cultural (e.g., spiritual and recreational values).

Section 7.2: Biodiversity and Ecosystem Services

The chapter explores the critical role of biodiversity in underpinning ecosystem services. It explains how diverse ecosystems, comprising a range of species, are more resilient and efficient in providing essential services that directly and indirectly contribute to food security.

Section 7.3: Pollinators and Crop Production

This section zooms in on the indispensable role of pollinators, such as bees and butterflies, in agriculture. It discusses the relationship between pollinator biodiversity and crop production, emphasizing the potential consequences of pollinator declines.

Section 7.4: Soil Health and Fertility

Soil is a fundamental resource for agriculture. This section elaborates on how healthy soil ecosystems, teeming with diverse microorganisms and invertebrates, play a pivotal role in maintaining soil fertility and providing essential nutrients for crops.

Section 7.5: Natural Pest Control

The chapter highlights the importance of natural pest control mechanisms provided by biodiversity-rich ecosystems. It discusses how beneficial insects and predators help control pest populations in agriculture, reducing the need for chemical pesticides.

Section 7.6: Water Resources and Food Security

The section delves into the relationship between ecosystems and water resources. It explains how healthy ecosystems, such as wetlands and forests, play a crucial role in regulating water flow, quality, and availability, which are all essential for food production.

Section 7.7: Cultural Ecosystem Services

The chapter concludes by acknowledging the cultural ecosystem services that nature provides, which contribute to the well-being and food security of communities. These services include spiritual and recreational values tied to biodiversity-rich environments.

Chapter 7 emphasizes the invaluable contributions of ecosystems and biodiversity to food security. It underscores the necessity of preserving these services by maintaining and restoring diverse natural environments, recognizing that a thriving natural world is the foundation for our ability to feed the planet.

8

Chapter 8: Agroecology: A Path to Biodiversity-Friendly Farming

This chapter delves into the principles and practices of agroecology, which offers a holistic and sustainable approach to agriculture that places a strong emphasis on preserving and enhancing biodiversity.

Section 8.1: What is Agroecology?

The section starts by defining agroecology, an approach to farming that draws from ecological principles. It emphasizes the importance of understanding local ecosystems, fostering biodiversity, and maintaining the health of both the environment and communities.

Section 8.2: Biodiversity at the Core

This section explores how agroecology places biodiversity at the core of agricultural practices. It emphasizes that diverse agroecological systems mimic natural ecosystems and capitalize on the interplay of different species to improve sustainability and resilience.

Section 8.3: Polyculture and Interplanting

The chapter discusses specific agroecological practices, such as polyculture and interplanting. These techniques involve growing multiple crop species together, promoting biodiversity in the field, and mimicking natural plant communities.

Section 8.4: Crop Rotation and Agroforestry

This section delves into crop rotation and agroforestry, two key strategies employed in agroecology. Crop rotation reduces the buildup of pests and diseases, while agroforestry integrates trees with crops, enhancing biodiversity and ecosystem services.

Section 8.5: Soil Health and Organic Practices

Agroecology places a strong emphasis on soil health. This section explains how organic and regenerative practices, such as composting, cover cropping, and reduced tillage, are pivotal in fostering biodiversity in the soil, which, in turn, supports crop growth.

Section 8.6: Case Studies in Agroecology

Readers are introduced to real-world case studies showcasing the success of agroecological practices. These examples highlight how farmers and communities have adopted agroecological techniques to improve food security while conserving biodiversity.

Section 8.7: Scaling Agroecology for Impact

The chapter concludes by addressing the challenges and opportunities in scaling up agroecology. It discusses the importance of policy support, farmer education, and community involvement in promoting this biodiversity-friendly approach to agriculture.

Chapter 8 shines a light on agroecology as a promising and practical path toward biodiversity-friendly farming. It underscores the potential of these principles and practices to address the pressing challenges of food security and environmental conservation, demonstrating that agriculture can be both productive and ecologically sustainable.

9

Chapter 9: Indigenous Knowledge and Biodiversity in Food Systems

This chapter delves into the invaluable role of indigenous knowledge in preserving biodiversity and promoting sustainable food systems.

Section 9.1: Indigenous Peoples and Biodiversity

The section begins by acknowledging the profound connection between indigenous peoples and their environments. It explores how indigenous communities have historically lived in harmony with nature, using traditional knowledge and practices to sustain biodiversity and food security.

Section 9.2: Traditional Crop Varieties and Livestock

Readers will gain insights into the diverse array of crop varieties and livestock breeds cultivated and raised by indigenous communities. These traditional varieties often exhibit high levels of biodiversity and are adapted to local environmental conditions.

Section 9.3: Local Food Systems and Biodiversity

The chapter highlights the significance of local food systems in preserving biodiversity. It discusses how indigenous communities often rely on diverse, locally adapted food sources, maintaining an essential connection between their culture and the land.

Section 9.4: Sustainable Land Management

Indigenous knowledge often encompasses sustainable land management practices. This section explores how indigenous communities employ techniques such as rotational farming, agroforestry, and watershed management to protect biodiversity and ensure food security.

Section 9.5: Cultural Practices and Food Security

The chapter delves into the cultural practices surrounding food and farming within indigenous communities. It emphasizes that these practices are not only about sustenance but also about maintaining cultural identity, social cohesion, and spiritual connections to the land.

Section 9.6: The Role of Traditional Knowledge in Modern Agriculture

The section concludes by considering the potential for integrating indigenous knowledge into modern agriculture and conservation efforts. It underscores the importance of respecting and partnering with indigenous communities to harness their wisdom for the benefit of biodiversity and global food security.

Chapter 9 provides a rich exploration of the profound contributions of indigenous knowledge to biodiversity preservation and sustainable food systems. It underscores the importance of acknowledging and respecting these traditional practices and partnering with indigenous communities in our collective efforts to address the challenges of agriculture and food security.

10

Chapter 10: Policy and Governance for Biodiversity and Food Security

In this chapter, we dive into the critical role of policies and governance structures in addressing the complex interplay between biodiversity and food security.

Section 10.1: The Need for Policy Frameworks

This section begins by emphasizing the necessity of comprehensive policy frameworks that address the challenges of biodiversity loss and food security. It outlines the ways in which these frameworks can set the stage for sustainable agricultural practices.

Section 10.2: National and International Agreements

The chapter discusses the significance of international agreements and conventions, such as the Convention on Biological Diversity (CBD) and the Sustainable Development Goals (SDGs). It explores how these global agreements establish targets and standards for biodiversity conservation and food security.

Section 10.3: Agricultural Policies and Incentives

This section delves into the specific agricultural policies and incentives that can either promote or hinder biodiversity-friendly farming. It emphasizes the importance of agricultural subsidies, land-use regulations, and incentives for sustainable practices.

Section 10.4: Local Governance and Community Engagement

The chapter highlights the role of local governance and community engagement in biodiversity and food security. It explains that local authorities and communities play a crucial role in shaping land-use decisions and sustainable practices.

Section 10.5: Integrated Approaches and Cross-Sectoral Policies

Integrated approaches that bridge various sectors, such as agriculture, environment, and trade, are vital. This section explores how cross-sectoral policies can address the multifaceted challenges of biodiversity and food security.

Section 10.6: Monitoring and Enforcement

The chapter concludes by addressing the importance of monitoring and enforcement of policies related to biodiversity and food security. It discusses the role of government agencies and non-governmental organizations in ensuring that policies are effectively implemented.

Chapter 10 underscores that sound policy and governance mechanisms are essential for creating an environment where agriculture and food security can coexist with biodiversity conservation. It explores the various levels at which policy decisions are made, from local to international, and how they shape the trajectory of our food systems and natural world.

11

Chapter 11: Technology and Innovation in Sustainable Agriculture

This chapter explores the role of cutting-edge technologies and innovative practices in promoting sustainable agriculture while conserving biodiversity.

Section 11.1: The Digital Revolution in Agriculture

The section begins by discussing the digital revolution in agriculture, focusing on the use of precision farming techniques, big data, and the Internet of Things (IoT) to optimize resource use, reduce environmental impact, and increase crop yields.

Section 11.2: Biotechnology and Genetic Resources

Readers will gain insights into the applications of biotechnology, including genetic modification and gene editing, in agriculture. The section also addresses the potential benefits and concerns related to biotechnology and its impact on biodiversity.

Section 11.3: Sustainable Farming Apps and Tools

The chapter highlights the proliferation of mobile apps and tools designed to support sustainable farming practices. These technologies provide farmers with real-time information and solutions for improving crop management and reducing environmental impact.

Section 11.4: Robotics and Automation in Agriculture

The section delves into the use of robotics and automation in agriculture, from autonomous tractors to precision weed control systems. It discusses how these technologies can enhance efficiency and reduce the need for chemical inputs.

Section 11.5: Innovative Sustainable Practices

In addition to high-tech innovations, this section explores low-tech and nature-based solutions that promote sustainability. It discusses practices such as agroforestry, no-till farming, and cover cropping, which contribute to biodiversity preservation and sustainable food production.

Section 11.6: Challenges and Ethical Considerations

The chapter concludes by addressing the challenges and ethical considerations related to adopting technology and innovation in agriculture. It emphasizes the importance of balancing technological advancements with ethical and ecological concerns.

Chapter 11 showcases the potential of technology and innovation to transform agriculture into a force for sustainability and biodiversity conservation. It recognizes that when harnessed thoughtfully and ethically, these advancements can contribute to more efficient and eco-friendly food production systems.

12

Chapter 12: Future Challenges and Opportunities for Food Security and Biodiversity

In this concluding chapter, we peer into the future, assessing the challenges that lie ahead and the opportunities to create a more harmonious and sustainable relationship between food security and biodiversity.

Section 12.1: Climate Change and Resilience

The section discusses the looming challenge of climate change and its profound impacts on both food security and biodiversity. It explores the need for adaptive strategies that enhance resilience in the face of shifting climate patterns.

Section 12.2: Population Growth and Food Demand

The chapter addresses the challenge of a growing global population and the increasing demand for food. It emphasizes the necessity of producing more food without exacerbating biodiversity loss.

Section 12.3: Sustainable Food Systems

This section examines the concept of sustainable food systems, which encompass the entire food supply chain, from production to consumption. It explores the potential for these systems to minimize waste, reduce environmental impact, and support both food security and biodiversity.

Section 12.4: The Role of Education and Advocacy

The chapter highlights the role of education and advocacy in shaping public perception and driving change. It underscores the importance of raising awareness and building support for sustainable food systems.

Section 12.5: The Promise of Technological Advancements

Readers will explore the potential of emerging technologies, such as vertical farming, cultured meat, and advanced aquaculture, in transforming food production systems and reducing environmental impacts.

Section 12.6: Global Collaboration and Policy

The chapter concludes by discussing the importance of global collaboration and strong policy frameworks. It emphasizes the role of international cooperation in addressing the challenges of food security and biodiversity on a worldwide scale.

Chapter 12 serves as a forward-looking reflection on the path ahead. It acknowledges the complex and intertwined challenges of providing food security for a growing population while preserving Earth's biodiversity. It also highlights the various opportunities, from innovative technologies to policy changes, that offer hope for a more sustainable future where both food security and biodiversity can thrive.